HOW TO BE FREE FROM EXCESS BAGGAGE

How To Be Free
From Excess Baggage

Copyright © 1998
Shiela Y. Harris
First Printing 2000

Unless otherwise indicated all Scripture quotations are taken from the HOLY BIBLE, NEW INTERNATIONAL VERSION®. Copyright © 1973, 1978, 1984 by International Bible Society. Used by permission of Zondervan Publishing House. All rights reserved.

The "NIV" and "New International Version" trademarks are registered in the United States Patent and Trademark Office by International Bible Society. Use of either trademark requires the permission of International Bible Society.

Scripture quotations marked KJV are taken from the King James Version of the Bible.

All rights reserved. No part of this publication may be reproduced, stored in a retrieval system or transmitted in any form or by any means, electronic, mechanical, photocopying, recording or otherwise, without the written permission from the author or publisher.

Printed by: Morris Publishing
3212 East Highway 30
Kearney, NE 68847
1-800-650-7888

ISBN: 0-9679312-0-2
Library of Congress Catalog Card Number: 00-90528

Dedication

To God who is the head of my life, Ted my husband and my best friend, to my pastors Melvin and April Jackson, my mentors and inspiration, my mother Ruth L. Green who has been a lifetime supporter and friend and to my children Denzil, Chisa and Damien.

INTRODUCTION

Many in the Body of Christ need deliverance from Excess Baggage. Not only lay persons but those in leadership as well. Bishops, pastors, elders, ministers, evangelist, missionaries and the like, whether or not they will admit it probably have excess baggage. The common practice is to function on a level that is considered normal by our peers while at the same time trying to cope while yet denying that baggage even exists. Deliverance is not experienced because pride and self-importance are key hindrances. Concerns of what others may think or how they will be viewed is a more important issue.

There are all sorts of issues that become our baggage, experiences from our childhood and from broken relationships and experiences from our past. Experiences and issues that you probably prefer not to think about. Issues that you want to keep buried in the past. Because of being preoccupied with how others might perceive them, believers in the Body of Christ are not always comfortable with admitting that they may need deliverance in any area of their lives.

Moreover, it is more probable that believers in the Body of Christ have not thought about the possibility that baggage even exists.

If you can set aside pride, position and status, this book will be a blessing to you because excess baggage on any level in ministry can and will hinder our walk with Christ as well as affect our relationships with others.

This book will truly bless you if your heart is receptive to what unfolds within. Your healing, deliverance and freedom lie within the pages as God reveals through the writer "How To Be Free From Excess Baggage."

Table of Contents

Dedication — iii

Introduction — v

Excess Baggage — xi

Chapter 1
What is Excess Baggage — 15

Chapter 2
Process of Elimination — 33

Chapter 3
Identifying Your Baggage — 49

Chapter 4
Guilt — 61

Chapter 5
Denial — 69

Chapter 6
Painful/Hurt — 77

Table of Contents

Chapter 7
    Know *Who* You Are in Christ   85

Chapter 8
    What Is Your Excess Baggage?   93

Chapter 9
    Be Free and Know It   105

Poem
    Who The Son Sets Free   111

About The Author   113

"So if the Son sets you free, you will be free indeed"

John 8:36 (N.I.V.)

Excess Baggage

Excess baggage is any experiences current or from your past that has tormented you and hindered your walk with Christ.

WHAT IS EXCESS BAGGAGE?

Chapter – 1

What Is Excess Baggage?

Excess Baggage is the result of unpleasant experiences and then the memory of these experiences tormenting you as they surface from time to time. Oftentimes you are aware of the experiences that become your baggage but it is also possible for you to be unaware that these experiences are the source. Nevertheless, unchecked excess baggage will control and dictate your behavior. You may realize that there is a problem and still not know its identity or source. From a spiritual standpoint excess baggage can and will hinder your walk with Christ, as well as impede all of life's relationships. When you are delivered from the affects of these experiences you release the power they have over you.

These experiences will control your actions and reactions. How you treat others, how you view others, whether you are paranoid or over trusting and whether you have a problem interacting with others. If you are one who is in and out of relationships, one who is in and out of marriages, a church hobo running from one ministry to another, or unstable in employment, you probably have excess baggage. The real problem is that you tend to think that it is everyone else who has a problem, and not you.

Excess Baggage is a powerful tool of the enemy. He uses baggage to mold your character, to distort your thinking causing you to lose spiritual focus. Your thoughts and ideals are hopeless and you are blinded from the truth of knowing what God's will is for your life.

Within the Body of Christ the people who have excess baggage are usually the ones who have trouble following leadership and working with others. They have difficulty yielding to anyone who has authority over them and seem to struggle when it comes to understanding the vision of the house. They are the ones who take up time in counseling sessions and seem to never really have any substantial growth spiritually. These leaders will usually have trouble with the structure and order that's set before them, they have trouble loving and working with difficult people and they have trouble leading by example and may even have difficulty leading people in general.

One of the characteristics of a person who carries excess baggage is there is always someone else to blame. It is in most cases, someone else's fault for the emotional state that they are in. They are disgruntled, miserable, unhappy souls. Even though they love God they just cannot seem to live life by the fruit of the Spirit.

The fruit of the Spirit is love, joy, peace, patience, kindness, goodness, faithfulness, gentleness and self-control. Galatians 5:22 (NIV)

If we are in Christ we are a new creature. The old habits and character traits that marked our lives before Christ are passing away. He makes us entirely new. So if we live by the Spirit we should walk in the Spirit. Conceit, proving one another, and envy cannot be a characteristic of a believer. If you possess spiritual qualities you can be at peace with yourself and then be empowered to impart these attributes to others and they will actually see this fruit in your daily walk.

It is possible that your excess baggage may have been caused at the hand of another but once we come into the knowledge of God and His Word, we cannot blame anyone else but ourselves for the emotional mess we allow ourselves to fall into behind excess baggage. You may have been a victim of rape, molestation, spousal abuse and these are all horrible and traumatic experiences, but as believers in Christ we also serve a God who can and will heal and deliver us from the pain and scars of our past.

When you recognize and identify the source of your baggage, it is up to you to allow God to deliver you from its bondage.

Let's look at Hebrews 12: 1-3:

"Wherefore seeing we also are compassed about with so great a cloud of witnesses, let us lay aside every weight, and the sin which doth so easily beset us, and let us run with patience the race that is set before us"(KJV).

..."Let us lay aside every weight," references the runners of that day. They would actually take off their clothes down to a loincloth. This procedure insured them that they would be able to run as fast as possible. *Lay aside every weight, and sin.* Every weight also symbolizes the excessive affection and concern we have for our body and the present life and world. Things that are also weights are things that keep us from serving God. It may be television, washing your car on Sundays, owning a car, feeling like you are the only one who can clean the church properly. When we have excessive concerns for our lives and the things of this world it changes our course from an upward direction to one of recession and failure. Excess baggage will result in your Christian walk being a lot more difficult than it should be. You must lay aside every hindrance (weight). Sometimes we already know what it is we need to strip off, what our weights are and sometimes it is oblivious to us. As you continue reading you will be able to recognize or identify your baggage.

When we are bound by baggage, whether it is a person or experience, blaming others does not eliminate the problem. Again, if you have allowed it to control your life you have you to blame. If you want to be angry with someone get angry at the devil and decide today that you are going to take back the control he has had over your life.

This book is going to help you release, and then be delivered from the source that brought the baggage into your life so that you can be totally free and know it. God cannot elevate us to higher levels in Him as long as we continue hiding under excess baggage. Say the following sentence out loud, "No more excess baggage!" Say it again, "No more excess baggage!"

Now you have made the devil real mad and that's good! We are children of a Holy and Righteous God and when we exercise the power he has given us as believers, the devil has to flee.

In order to release your baggage you need to know the source. There may be people you need to release and the source can be one or many experiences. The following is a personal experience of mine that I would like to share with you because

I believe it may be helpful. There was some dissension between myself and a member in our ministry. The manner in which this member handled our differences was totally wrong. As a result of malice, and the lies being told to numerous people, from time to time I still hear the negative talk that resulted from what was said. But what is more important, I allowed this person to become a source of baggage. Finally, I had to realize (and I believe this is why God gave this to me – to help me first) that my reactions towards this person were affecting others in the ministry. Even though people who witnessed my reactions were not privileged to the whole truth of the matter, it was more important for me to stop trying to make a wrong right, and to not hold a grudge, nor let this situation hinder my walk with Christ. In ministry and in every area of your life people are watching you, especially when you profess Christ. The saved and the unsaved watch your daily walk. Some watch us because they are impressed by the Jesus they see in us while others watch us because they are impressed by what they do not see.

My reaction was that of anger and a "get even spirit". It was more important to me at the time that the people knew that the talk was a lie. But in order for anyone to know the whole truth of the matter I would have to resort to gossiping which would consequently make bad matters even worse. Negatively dealing with my anger and having a "get even spirit" drew my focus away from God. After a while, people could predict how I would react and they began to dig up "bones" and bring them to me. You know the old cliché "misery loves company." We should be aware that people are not interested in our well being when they bring us garbage but they are more interested in stirring up trouble. Those who love God and believe His Word should not yield to gossip. This means we should not gossip nor listen to it.

One Sunday morning during the message one of my senior pastors made a statement, she said, "All one has to do to be vindicated from a lie is to out live it." God spoke directly to my spirit during that message and I heard Him loud and clear. It was as if someone slapped me upside my head and turned on the light of conviction. It was in my best interest to *let it go* and to forgive the transgressor and love them the way Christ loves me. The process of forgiveness did not happen over night, but once I recognized this was baggage and realized how it was affecting my spiritual walk, I let it go. Our paths still cross from time to time and while they yet refuse to even speak to me God revealed to me that for my spiritual well being, I must love and release the person as well as the lies. My God, release? Easier said then done! But it had to be done. If we are going to profess Christ we must possess his attributes. It is all the way with him or no way, there is no in between.

There have been other events in my life that I could share that became my excess baggage but this book would be filled with nothing but baggage stories if I tried to share them all. But there is one more experience I feel is important to share because it was through this experience even as painful and devastating as it was that I received total deliverance. In sharing this I pray that it will help you as you overcome your excess baggage.

How To Be Free From Excess Baggage

In a very shocking and heart-wrenching manner my marriage of almost nineteen years was ripped apart. Up to this point the relationship had began to get rocky but in no way was I prepared for the events that eventually led to the dissolution of the marriage. My spouse was a respected man and we both were very involved in ministry. It was the kind of relationship, even with its rocky moments people admired. Many thought we were the ideal couple. I had reason to be suspicious but no real evidence that he was having an extramarital affair. Especially since the affair was with one of the members in the same ministry that we both attended. To compound things even more it was about this same time I discovered that he had also been accused of molesting one of my children, both allegations of which he admitted to. Other matters of deceit and malice began to unfold and it resulted in a nasty divorce, which led to the loss of my home, ruined credit, and stress began to swallow me whole both physically and emotionally. Our children were emotionally scarred and this of course became big time baggage, which made it difficult for me to have any future, healthy relationships. For me, there could not and would not be any more trust in a man. All men were scandalous in my eyesight, not to be trusted. Slowly the bitterness and pain began to destroy me from the inside out.

As the enemy began to slowly take control I can remember being overly negative about any and everything, my overall relationship with people in general began to suffer. This and other experiences hindered my spiritual walk because I allowed them to be my "excess baggage." The responsibility for the bad things that happened to me did not lie with me, but I was responsible for allowing the enemy to control my actions. I was even trying to help God work out my problems and he definitely did not need any help from me. The importance of not allowing life's disappointments to stand between you and God cannot be stressed enough. Things happen! But we cannot let these things cause us to lose sight of God.

Some of my problems were because of a lack of spiritual knowledge. Even though I had been in the church all of my life I had not been filled with the Holy Ghost. This gift as well as other spiritual gifts were not a part of the teaching in the ministry I was apart of at that time. There was a hunger for more of God but I was hindered because of a lack of spiritual knowledge. My spiritual weapons and resources were limited and the enemy of course knew this.

I remember even before this experience that there was a spiritual void or hunger and these events as traumatic as they were drew me closer to God. As I began to listen to His voice He led me to a church where the five-fold ministry gifts are in full manifestation and the ministry's foundation is built on Bible principles. In this place I was taught that the baptism of the Holy Ghost is essential if we want to experience the Glory of God and receive His benefits and thus beginning the divesting ourselves of our excess baggage.

You may find that there are experiences you need to release. Rape or molestation, easily identifiable and abusive acts. Maybe you experienced years of continuous mental abuse. The abuse could have been indirect you may have witnessed the constant abuse of another (your dad beating your mother, your mom beating your siblings). These things not only have a psychological effect but they can be emotionally devastating as well.

Psychological problems do not necessarily mean that you are crazy but you can have trouble functioning normally because of how these traumas affect the mental and spiritual balance you need in life to be whole.

Christians will often go to psychiatrist to help them cope with their psychological and emotional problems, and in no way am I against physicians, Luke was a physician. But excess baggage is like an acute infection and it "infects" your mental and spiritual stability. From a spiritual perspective, psychiatrists don't have an antidote for this kind of illness. There is no prescription or antibiotic that can cure spiritual illness. More importantly, psychiatrist cannot free your soul; mind intellect and emotions. The only way you can truly be set free is through being saved (sozo in the Greek) and receiving deliverance through Jesus Christ. The word "sozo" means to be saved, healed, preserved, delivered and made whole.

There have been many claims to fame and sovereignty but Jesus demonstrated that He was God by His words and actions. He healed the sick, raised the dead, forgave sins, and lived by the moral precepts that He taught. In fact, he fulfilled every code of righteousness without ever sinning. More importantly, he backed up his claim of being God when He conquered death. No one can match God's glory but Jesus and they are one.

The bible says in John 8:36:

"So if the son sets you free you are free indeed." (KJV)

The Greek word for free is *eleuteros,* which means to set free from the dominion (power) or bondage of sin. The Greek word for indeed is *ontous* meaning you are absolutely free. This is another reason why we find so many people up one day and down the next. They never get totally delivered, when God sets you free, you better believe you are free!

We need a spiritual intervention when it comes to getting rid of excess baggage. If baggage is continuously ignored it continues to fester while tormenting you as it surfaces over and over again (just like garden weeds that are never attacked at the root).

As you read through this book and resolve in yourself to be totally honest, you will find that you need to release some excess baggage. In order for us to walk in our destiny, we must let go of pride and haughtiness. As long as there is baggage weighing us down we will not walk in God's will.

Depending on your position you are probably thinking that you are an astute man or woman of God, Holy Ghost filled...and so what! You can still have baggage. Oftentimes pride accompanies positions and titles, but baggage has no respect of person, position or title. Evangelists and missionaries, pastors and elders, ministers and officers, no one is exempt because of status or position.

There are all sorts of excess baggage. You may be angry with your father who you never really knew for walking out on you, and for physically and mentally abusing you. You could be angry with your parents for dragging you through their divorce and leaving you with emotional scars. Your baggage could be from many sources, the betrayal of a best friend even in ministry. If you reflect with an honest and open heart you will find that baggage is there. We are going to discuss and deal with this in a later chapter.

Before we go any further you must let down the barriers of pride so the message in this book can bless you. It neither makes a difference who you are or what your status is. None of this is important, but what does matter is who you are about to become. None of this matters, your past is not important to God. Where you have been is not as important as where you are going, not your history but your destiny. As we deal with the "whole" you, your body, emotions, mind, mouth, will, attitude and spirit, you are on your way to complete freedom from the hindrances and bondage of excess baggage.

PROCESS OF ELIMINATION

Chapter – 2

Process of Elimination

There are four processes you need to work through before you can release excess baggage. These processes include identifying the baggage, identifying the source, releasing the weight and pain and finally to be "FREE" and KNOW it.

Think about this for a moment. What or who has you weighed down? Is it from your childhood? Is it from a past relationship? As Christians we often try to display ourselves as super heroes. We think we are faster than the devil, more powerful than God, and able to leap tall problems in a single bound. Duh! We are not invincible. Problems do not just, "go away!" Whether you will admit it or not, you know the baggage is there because its weight continues to surface, cutting through your emotions like a two-edged sword. One edge makes you remember the source while the other will not let you forget the pain.

Look at this scenario. A woman is really in love with and devoted to her husband but finds her marriage going sour and her mate is no longer in love with her. He no longer desires to spend the next day with her, forget spending the rest of their lives together. He is a physically abusive man and a compulsive gambler who is also intimately involved with several women outside their marriage. While we are on the subject, God did not create women to be abused and misused, we do not have to stay and we should not be expected to stay in physically abusive relationships.

But what happens in a situation like this? How does this experience become her baggage? She is saved, she knows God, so how does excess baggage become a controlling part of her life?

One reason is that the enemy knows our weaknesses and when our focus is on the pain or problem, which is induced by the baggage, it is an avenue for him to move in. If loneliness or rejection is a weakness, the enemy sends this our way. He knows what buttons to push to cause us to lose our focus and deviate from the things of God to the sources of baggage.

Let's continue with our scenario. A year has passed and she thinks she is over him and for the time being she is coping. Holiday's roll around and she feels deserted and alone. There are times she feels left out and cheated and she reflects back on her failed relationship. The crying begins and she is an emotional wreck. She hides it well and no one knows about these emotional bouts with her past, nobody but she and God. These episodes become a pattern and she is constantly on an emotional roller coaster. The mood swings are predictable and with each episode the intensity heightens. She resigns herself to believing this situation to be something that will pass with time and she also believes that when these episodes come she can deal with them. She even believes that surely all hurting women experience this, don't they? Don't we all have our share of pity parties?

She attends church regularly, except for when the emotional episodes come upon her. It is good that she attends church regularly but it is so sad that there is never any real deliverance. There is nothing wrong with the ministry she is in the problem lies within her. After each service she leaves the same way she came in bound to baggage. It is difficult to enter into praise and worship or to receive from God. Her excess baggage causes the simple things in her life to be challenging.

This is just one example of how the enemy can get a grip on you. Whatever way he can get in is fine with him, just as long as he gets in. If it is emotionally that is fine. He can destroy from any angle all he has to do is get in. This is why it is so important that we identify the source. Identify how this baggage got into our life but this process is not always easy. The sources are sometimes gray areas and aside from them surfacing at will you try not to think about them at all. This is your way of coping, your way of survival, by ignoring or simply trying to forget that you have a problem.

Since the source of your baggage is neither pleasant nor comfortable to think about, how does one reflect on things like your uncle molesting you when you were a child and keep their sanity? Maybe their father physically abused them for breakfast, lunch and dinner. Perhaps relatives teased you because of your complexion being darker or lighter than others in the family. If anything, we try very hard to forget these things. To wish them into the sea of "bad things be gone." It is just too painful to remember.

Be assured in knowing that as you read this book and are encouraged to remember these things, this will be the last time, this or any other baggage will torment you. In a later chapter there will be an exercise for you to do to help you identify your baggage and then you will be shown how to receive, "right now" deliverance. Hallelujah! Glory to God! My God you are going to be free!

Stay with me and you are on your way to complete deliverance and freedom from your excess baggage.

The next step after you identify the source is to release the weight and pain. Baggage weighs you down and keeps you from experiencing the fullness of God. This has nothing to do with you being filled with His precious Holy Spirit but it does keep you from enjoying all the benefits of the believer. Not so you say? Well let's see.

You go to church and try to enter in His presence during praise and worship. There is difficulty in getting an audience with God because your thought patterns are baggage controlled and are weighing you down. Your mind should be on God but you keep reflecting on your ex-husband or ex-wife who is in a new relationship and they are now worshipping in the same ministry. My God, they just walked in with their newly found love! Or maybe you had a misunderstanding with one of the sisters or one of the brothers and they just sat next to you (you are not on speaking terms). Oh, and what about holidays, take Father's Day and Mother's Day for an example, you have a heavy heart because you have not released a parent that preceded you in death. Your praise and worship is not true praise and worship it is more from an emotional position rather than from a spiritual one. Can you truly worship and praise God in spite of or does the baggage get in the way?

You even find that you cannot comfortably work in any area of ministry because you are one of those who have been hurt and you are "waiting on direction." There are 101 things within the ministry that need to be done and none of these needs seem to be your calling. You cannot hear your calling because the voice of your baggage is louder than the voice of God. You will be waiting and waiting because your baggage is going to continue to hinder your walk with Christ. There will not be any real peace or comfort for you until you release the weight and pain and receive complete deliverance.

Notice I said you must "release it." God is not going to take it from you until you willingly hand it over to him. God is a perfect gentleman and He is not going to hold you down and beat you over the head and force you to release your baggage. He will wait on you until you are ready to give it up. It is then and only then that God can freely move on your behalf freeing your spirit from bondage. When you give it up, Satan has to go and take his baggage with him. Once we give it up and hand it over to God it will no longer surface and torment us. Lastly, you will be FREE and KNOW it. You are going to experience this freedom as you continue reading the later chapters. Even now God is working on your behalf. The enemy is shaking because that rascal knows he does not have much time in your vessel. In the name of Jesus, he is going to have to loose you! Repeat this sentence aloud, *"Satan, I am serving notice on you, so get your baggage packed because in the name of Jesus you MUST go!"* Say it again and say it like you mean it! This is our baggage check and we will use this throughout the remainder of this book. When I say, " baggage check," you repeat this statement aloud and mean it.

Let's look at John 8:36. Actually let us begin at verse 31 and go through to verse 36:

"Then said Jesus to those Jews which believed on him, If ye continue in my word, then are ye my disciples indeed; And ye shall know the truth, and the truth shall make you free. They answered him, We are Abraham's seed, and were never in bondage to any man: how sayest thou, Ye shall be made free? Jesus answered them, Verily, verily, I say unto you; whosoever committeth sin is the servant of sin. And the servant abideth not in the house forever: but the Son abideth forever. If the Son therefore shall make you free, ye shall be free indeed. (KJV)

The Greek word for free is eleuteros and means to set free from the dominion or bondage of sin. The eighth chapter of John records a very heated, even bitter confrontation between Jesus and the Jews led by the Pharisees dealing with spiritual liberty. Christ became particularly curt with the religious leaders because they refused to accept His claims, jeopardizing not only their own spiritual standing but also that of Israel. Jesus was offering discipleship or spiritual freedom to those who would believe on Him. God not only speaks to those who tremble at his word and are ready to receive it but to those also who have hearing ears and set themselves in his way. We find that these Jews were so pompous they missed the whole concept or premise of the conversation.

If we believe on Christ we are his disciples. The truth that Christ teaches makes us free. It makes us free from our spiritual enemies, free in the service of God.

These carnal Jews took offense because they figured since they were descendants of Abraham's seed they were born into freedom. So they questioned Christ as to what he meant by they shall be made free. They were borrowing from their ancestor's dignity to which they disgraced. So they did not believe they needed to have faith in Christ to be free. But they failed to realize that the seed of Abraham was once in bondage to the Egyptians and during the time of the Judges they were in bondage to Babylon for 70 years. And even at this time they were tributaries to the Romans and were in a national bondage to them.

Jesus Christ offers us our freedom and he has the authority and power to make us free. Through sanctification he rescues the bound. By the powerful operations of his spirit he breaks the power of corruption in the soul and fortifies God's interest against sin and Satan, and the soul is made free. We are forgiven and healed. The liberty that Christ gives is certain and we are *free*.

This is what you need, spiritual freedom. A one-time rescue where you know that without any doubt your baggage can no longer hold you bound in its destructive grip.

We have God's Word to teach and direct us so we are not bound to things that are opposite his word. In Romans 6-8 chapters, Paul discusses the working out of the Gospel in a Christian's life. Paul does not say that only good or pleasurable things will come to us.

Look at Romans 8: 35-39:

Who shall separate us from the love of Christ? Shall trouble or hardship or persecution or famine or nakedness or danger or sword? As it is written: "For your sake we face death all day long; we are considered as sheep to be slaughtered." No, in all these things we are more than conquerors through him who loved us. For I am convinced that neither death nor life, neither angels nor demons, neither the present nor the future, nor any powers, neither height nor depth, nor anything else in all creation, will be able to separate us from the love of God that is in Jesus Christ our Lord. (NIV)

Believers are not promised immunity from this world's problems and pain. Everyday we have to be exposed to the good as well as the evil. But good can come out of bad. God uses all situations in our lives, the good and the bad for his purpose in us. Remember that His purpose can only be good. So as we face troubled times we must assert our trust in God's presence, lineup our goals with God's principles which will lead us to our purpose as we accept and believe the promises of God. These difficult experiences can be used in God's overall plan for good, and knowing this nothing can separate us from the love of God. The chapter begins with no condemnation and it ends with no separation and in between there is no defeat. God does not condemn us, he does not separate himself from us and in him there is victory.

Also in Romans Chapter 8, Paul defines the Spirits role in our lives. The Spirit works alongside us as we relate to God, even praying for us when we don't know what to ask. Romans 8: 26-27:

"In the same way, the Spirit helps us in our weakness. We do not know what we ought to pray for, but the Spirit Himself intercedes for us with groans that words cannot express. And he who searches our hearts knows the mind of the Spirit,

because the Spirit intercedes for the saints in accordance with God's will. (NIV)

God has equipped every believer for every trial. He will not put more on us than we are capable of bearing. We must have faith, believe God for victory before we receive it, and the Holy Spirit will teach and direct us as we draw closer to Him.

Now! With all this power and with God's Spirit working on the behalf of every believer, what happens to cause us to become separated? I am glad you asked! Sin separates us from God. Baggage is a form of sin and it can and will come between your relationship with God when we allow the enemy to torment us, control our thoughts and take our focus away from the things of God.

One last thing before we go on. It is possible that baggage as in the case of believers in Christ, for the most part, was acquired before we received our Salvation, and it is possible that it has festered on the inside for many, many years. Baggage can also be from current events or experiences that occurred after we are saved. I am aware that some astute scholars will probably disagree because of

How To Be Free From Excess Baggage

their own personal impairment induced through traditionalism and religion and as mentioned earlier position and status creates blinders and it makes this not applicable to all. But as was mentioned baggage has no respect of person or position. There may be all sorts of reason you may find as to why there has not been any real change or total deliverance in your life but it is not at all a mystery but very simple, you never went through this process of elimination. Remember, this process includes recognizing and identifying the baggage and its source, releasing the weight and pain and then to be FREE - and KNOW it!

IDENTIFYING YOUR BAGGAGE

Chapter – 3
Identifying Your Baggage

For some the baggage may be obvious but for others it may not be. It is important that you identify your baggage so you know without any doubt what it is you need deliverance from. Think about how awkward it feels to carry luggage. Luggage is clumsy, heavy, and cumbersome. Even with the luxury of the modern day slim-line styles with rollers the baggage is still cumbersome. Try this little exercise. Pick up a briefcase or a small piece of luggage and try to praise God. You won't last long. You may move a few steps and jump once or twice but holding on to that briefcase makes your praise more of a challenge because you will find that your thoughts are on the weight and awkwardness of the luggage. Baggage works the same in a spiritual sense. The concept is the same. Your mind is weighed down and confused and it becomes difficult to focus. Your soul man - mind, intellect and emotions - are warring and praise as well as worship becomes a challenge. God promises to give us perfect peace if our minds are continuously on him.

"Peace I leave with you, my peace I give unto you; not as the world giveth, give I unto you. Let not your heart be troubled neither let it me afraid." John 14:27. (KJV)

We cannot experience the peace of God when we are constantly struggling with baggage. We live in a disturbed world and change is much faster and more climatic than ever before. Some baggage is too painful to identify and you may not want to be reminded. It is hard enough dealing with it when it surfaces from time to time but not dealing with it at all will not make it disappear. Jesus alone is the only one that can give us perfect peace to help us live with virtue and wholeness.

After my marriage hit the rocks I can remember how I thought everything was under control. I resolved that the next man that came into my life was going to catch holy hell. I was going to be a witch on wheels. No trust, no love, no being faithful. He would be the victim, being used by me until I used him up and then wait patiently for my next victim. My new philosophy was don't give love, don't expect love and you won't get hurt.

My summation of the male species was that all men were jerks without a loyal or faithful bone in their bodies. They all played the field, they were all lustful, over-sexed creatures that could not and would not seek satisfaction in being with, or faithful to "one" woman. Was I messed up? Of course I was! I even tried to convince myself that there was no desire in my heart to ever be involved in another serious relationship. No way! No how!

Even though my pain was real the problem was not in men but in me. I allowed the enemy to steal my joy. He controlled my thoughts and emotions and challenged my faith. When I should have been looking at the promises of God my focus was on the problems. When we take our eyes off Christ we lose sight of Him and his purpose for our lives. His purpose is replaced with confusion, pain, defeat, hurt, revenge and resentment.

Praise God these things are buried in the past and once your baggage is released you too will have a clearer and closer relationship with Christ. You will begin to seek after the things of God based on

Biblical principals and directed by his Spirit who is within each of us.

One of the main problems we encounter after identifying that we have baggage as well as a problem we have with God delivering us from our excess baggage is that we just do not believe that He will. Some of us believe that He "can," but don't believe He "will". We have been delivered from one thing but don't believe God will deliver us from something else. It is as though we have been allotted a certain amount of things that God will deliver us from. He delivered you from smoking but He can't deliver you from drinking. He delivered you from fear but He cannot deliver you from gossip. That is a dressed up trick of the enemy. If the devil can get us to waiver in our Faith he can get us to believe almost anything.

Lastly, if excess baggage is not identified it limits your successes. It hinders you in the natural. On your job, in daily relationships with your colleagues and peers, how you relate with family and the list goes on and on. People can no longer see the Jesus in you for the pain and hurt.

Baggage also limits your spiritual successes because you are no longer in a position to receive the blessings of God. Excess baggage spiritually disables you and prevents you from walking with a godly boldness. This is not to be confused with walking in a spirit of control or deceit but being able to perform your day-to-day tasks without fear and inhibitions. No matter how successful you may think you are when under the bondage of baggage it will control and limit your successes. You cannot walk in prophetic destiny but instead you walk in the flesh on a road of spiritual destruction. Baggage check!

During our travels no matter what mode of transportation we use, we are usually issued a claim check to be used to identify luggage. Because people forget to claim their baggage everyday there is a lot that goes unclaimed just sitting in a lost and found area for an indefinite period. So it is with the baggage in our lives, we just walk around with the claim check but we fail to identify it and it becomes a part of our lives for indefinite periods of time.

Look at 2 Corinthians 5:17:

"Therefore, if anyone is in Christ, he is a new creation; the old has gone, the new has come!" (NIV)

When we become saved our Salvation gives us a clean slate. No matter what happened in our past, the day we accept Jesus as our Lord and Savior we become new creatures in Him. Christ does not push rewind and he does not have to use instant replay. He is a God of a second chance. Hallelujah! Praise God! But our happiness and joy in this new life depends a lot on us. The benefits are here for us but we must claim them in Jesus' name. Deliverance is yours. Healing is yours. Peace is yours. Success and prosperity is yours.

When baggage is left unclaimed it can and will destroy you, your spirit, soul and body, limit your successes as mentioned before, feeds low self-esteem and gives a sense of false security.

Your mind, intellect and emotions become infected and this infection stands between you and your relationship with God. The first time your pastor walks by and does not speak to you, or forgets to publicly call your name, you take it personal because you are insecure. You may even question your own self worth. You can be a minister or a leader in the ministry and have hang-ups because you feel you are not being recognized for your enumerate abilities. You feel lonely and unloved, feel you are being ignored and left out. Some get angry because their pastors do not have the time to counsel with them week after week for the same thing over and over. We are not in ministry to be constantly nursed as babies not yet weaned from their mother's breast but to be fed so that we can grow in Christ and win others to Christ. Our local ministry is not about us. It is only about God. All the glory, honor, credit, it all belongs to God.

Baggage can keep you from having a complete relationship with God. It will stand in between you and God and keep you from feeding your spirit the things of God. You will even find it difficult to genuinely love others and baggage will keep you from letting others love you. Love is an attribute of God, look at 1 John 4: 7-13:

Dear friends let us love one another, for love comes from God. Everyone who loves has been born of God and knows God. Whosoever does not love does not know God, because God is love. This is how God showed his love among us; he sent his one and only son into the world, that we might live through him. This is love: Not that we loved God, but that he loved us and sent his son as an atoning sacrifice for our sins. Dear friends, since God so loved us, we also ought to love one another. No one has ever seen God, but if we love one another, God lives in us and his love is made complete in us. We know that we live in him and he in us, because he has given us of his spirit. (NIV)

If God has given us His Spirit, not being able to truly love someone keeps you from having a complete relationship with Him. Baggage can prevent us from receiving love and giving love. You cannot give away something you don't have. Joyce Meyer said in her book, "How To Succeed in Being Yourself," "If you don't have love you cannot give it, if you don't receive God's mercy you can't be merciful to others." This is why we often react out of anger instead of out of love because we do not know real love, the love of God as when he gave his one and only son to die in atonement for our sin.

Unidentified baggage also results in low self-esteem, which ultimately leads to dependence on false securities. You will be drawn into abusive relationships, drug and alcohol usage and socializing with ungodly people. You set yourself up for failure. You have very little or no self pride and consequently you feed into people with the same mind, and into situations that keep you down because baggage has you thinking you cannot do better, or that you do not deserve better. It is very important that your baggage is identified so you can begin the process of elimination.

How To Be Free From Excess Baggage

GUILT

Chapter – 4

Guilt…

One thing we need to discuss before we go any further is GUILT. Guilt is defined as the state of having done a wrong or committed an offense; a painful feeling of self-reproach resulting from a belief that one has done something wrong or immoral.

The source of your baggage can cause feelings of guilt, even in situations where you were the one violated. Guilt is another destructive tool of the enemy. It is designed to bring about self-destruction. When you carry feelings of guilt you cannot feel spiritually secure. Sometimes you may even doubt your Salvation. There may be thoughts of your own self worth causing you to feel as though you do not deserve the better things in life. If bad things are happening to you, your thoughts may be that this is happening because of past deeds. Guilt keeps you bound to your past and will not let you forgive yourself. You cannot receive God's forgiveness if you cannot forgive yourself.

Guilt is the cause of self-condemnation for current and past behaviors. Maybe you have been convicted for a past sin and now it has become your baggage. If you have repented God has forgiven you but you just cannot seem to let go and forgive yourself. Self-forgiveness can be difficult because people won't let you forget. You are required to indicate on employment applications all prior convictions. You are ostracized by family, friends and sometimes even in the church. We continue to bring the past into our present causing us to ride an emotional roller coaster.

As believers in Christ we must apply the Word of God to our lives daily. He is our guide. Through daily Bible study and through the revelation knowledge God gives us in His Word, we learn what God's will is for our lives. I referred to this earlier and I will refer to it again, God loved us so much that He gave us His only son Jesus in sacrifice for our SIN. He loved us so much that He gave His life on the cross that His redemptive work might be complete. John 3:16-18:

"For God so loved the world that he gave his one and only son, that whosoever believes in him shall not perish but have eternal life. For God did not send his son into the world to condemn the world, but to save the world through him. Whosoever believes in him is not condemned, but whoever does not believe stands condemned already because he has not believed in the name of God's one and only son." (NIV)

There is no greater love than this. God does not condemn us so stop condemning yourself. You must stop letting the world condemn you. The only condemnation we stand in is if we do not believe in the Name of Jesus Christ. It is by God's grace that we are saved. Salvation is a precious gift of God, through Jesus Christ our Lord. It does not matter what your past has been. You don't have to try and explain or justify your sin. Jesus took our place on the cross in atonement for our sin. If there has been transgression, God sees sin as sin. Because of who you are in Christ you have no more or no less grace than the next person does, according to your faith in Him.

When you are weighed down with guilt you see yourself as a failure. You cannot see yourself as someone God would use. Guilt makes us play "rewind" on the annals of our lives. Past experiences overpower us and control our every thought.

Remorsefulness is also very common in victims of rape or molestation. The trauma can leave one with annoying thoughts of being at fault, left feeling ashamed and worthless. Look at John 10:10:

"The thief cometh not, for to steal, and to kill, and to destroy: I am come that they might have life, and that they might have it more abundantly." (KJV)

It is the enemy's job to try to destroy us and he will do so by any means necessary. Excess baggage can and will destroy you. So as you identify the baggage and source, as you release the weight and pain you must also release yourself from ALL guilt. Just in case you have not asked God to forgive you let's do it now. Say this prayer aloud:

"Dear Lord, I come humbly before you asking you to forgive me for all unrighteousness. Give me a clean heart and renew my spirit so I might serve you. Remove the guilt and pain so I may receive forgiveness, in Jesus' name I pray. Amen."

Now that you have repented and asked God for forgiveness believe in your heart that it is done. You have been pardoned to go and sin no more, go and feel guilty no more! *Baggage check!*

It is up to you whether you will live free from guilt and shame or live eternally tormented. Remember that our deliverance depends on us. It depends on our perspectives of the past and our perception of the now. The Bible reads in 2 Timothy 1:7:

"For God did not give us the spirit of timidity (fear) but a spirit of power, of love and of self-discipline (sound mind)." (NIV)

You must remember, whenever fear or guilt arises it is not the Spirit of God and you need to begin rebuking those thoughts. When our minds become open vessels, tools that the enemy can use, he uses it. He puts in thoughts of destruction, thoughts of defeat and fear. We know it is the devil because God has not given us the spirit of fear. We belong to God and no weapon formed against us shall prosper. God has given us divine power through Jesus Christ to defeat the attacks of the enemy. It is up to us to exercise that power.

"No, in all these things we are more than conquerors through him who loved us.
Romans 8: 37 (NIV)

So no matter what we face from day to day we are more than conquerors. No more guilt!

DENIAL

Chapter – 5
Denial

Take a few moments and reflect on a time when you were traveling various roads in the city. I am certain you will recall being detoured by a road block or road closure. A barrier or detour sign is placed on the road to prevent traveling past a certain point. Excess baggage causes you to travel to a closed or blocked road, which we will call "denial." The dictionary defines denial as *a refusal to accept.* When one is in denial they refuse to accept or they reject the actual truth. When we travel the road of denial we allow life's situations, or things we want, even when we know they are not good for us to stand in the way of our destiny. Our vision becomes clouded with what we see is a need rather than seeing what is really best for us.

I have taken the word denial and broken it down using each letter d-e-n-i-a-l to explain how denial can lead to destruction.

Look at the first letter which is "D", this represents *disparity*. Disparity means that something is unequal, it does not balance out. The baggage you are carrying is not a real part of you and it causes an imbalance in your life, especially in your spiritual life. Disparity acts much like a parasite. A parasite is an organism that lives on or within another organism called the host and it gains its sustenance from the host organism without any real benefit to the host. In other words we become the host for disparity. It keeps us holding on to our excess baggage while keeping us unbalanced, causing us to constantly be in a state of denial. Baggage becomes your parasite. It sucks the life right out of you.

Next, look at "E," *escaping reality*. Escape means to get free; to get away from; to get out. In this case, to brake free from reality. You do not see things as they really are. Your world is one of fabrication and there may even be laughter on the outside but on the inside there is pain and turmoil. The experiences that created your baggage are real and not necessarily your fault. But we cannot live in denial we must face things head on and see things for what they really are. We do not have to accept these negative things but we do have to face them. Once we face the reality of things, even when it is painful to do so, our baggage can be more readily released. It is not healthy to continuously suppress things because baggage does not just go "poof be gone." Without complete deliverance it will surface over and over again. Before you realize it much of your life's time and energy is spent escaping the reality of things.

The letter "N", *not at all true*. When we carry baggage we have a propensity to deal in untruths. We grasp things that give a false sense of security things like drugs, alcohol or abusive relationships. We delight ourselves in gossip, the business of others, and we even make public our own personal business. We involve ourselves in things that are untruths. *Not at all true* will drag you to the bottom of the barrel with the rest of the crabs, and you will continuously be trying to fight your way up and out, stepping on all that get in your way. Not at all true, is not at all healthy.

We are still discussing denial and the letter "I" represents *inconsistency*, you are self-contradictory. You may find yourself not holding true to Biblical principles and practices that you earnestly believe in. Excess baggage not only weighs you down but it causes confusion. You are not really sure what you believe in nor why you believe it. This type of insecurity indicates there are illogical thoughts continuously dancing around in your head.

Ambivalence represents the letter "A". The life you choose to live is contradictory to the Word, whether it is in your choice of friends, mates or personal involvement. The Bible warns us against being unequally yoked, but we are so hard up for relationship we take the first "jabo" or "bimbo" that comes our way. You may even find your life is one grave discrepancy because you have the ability to feel attraction and repulsion towards objects, persons and actions at the same time. There is always uncertainty as to which approach to follow.

The last letter is "L" and it represents a *lie*. This does not need a lot of explanation. A lie is simply something that is not true and being in denial means there is no real truth in your life.

Overall, denial is dangerous. Over long periods of time not knowing how to be free, you start to believe you need your baggage. You feel your life is not complete without this baggage. Denial fuels your moods, zaps your energy and dictates whether your life is one of failure or one of success. You are convinced that you do not want to live without it and will not admit that you need to release the person or source of your baggage. *Baggage check!*

Let me remind you of an assurance we find in Isaiah 26:3:

You will keep in perfect peace him whose mind is steadfast, because he trust in you. (NIV)

When you find yourself having detoured onto the road of denial focus on Christ. There is perfect peace in Him regardless of how things may look. The dread and gloom cannot occupy a mind that is pre-occupied with Christ.

How To Be Free From Excess Baggage

PAINFUL / HURT

Chapter – 6

Painful…Hurt

A few of my past, painful experiences has been discussed in previous chapters, as well as how God delivered me from the baggage I carried. Up to this point I have not shared anything about my current life. I'm blessed beyond measure. Happily married to my husband Ted Harris who is a kind, loving, thoughtful man of God. Highly involved in ministry he serves as Executive Pastor to the Senior Pastors in the Believers' Christian Ministries. We have truly learned the value of trusting God and being patient as He prepares us to do His will. Ted is a God fearing man and he treats me like a Nubian Princess. He loves respects and honors me. We work together as a team in ministry and truly enjoy working together and being with each other. Because of my hurting past it took me some time to get to a place of trust and thank God this was accomplished before we said, "I do." Ted is patient and loving, and it was during these times that God had me realize that there was excess baggage in my life. There was no level of trust because of constant deceit over such a long period of time in the past by people I trusted. I had not realized just how much paranoia and insecurity lay inside me.

As I previously mentioned, there was very little trust on my part. I wanted him to carry a beeper, cell phone and leave a daily itinerary. Sounds funny and ridiculous and it never came to that but I was that insecure. When someone betrays your trust, unless you are delivered you feel no one is trustworthy. You tend to make false accusations implicating one in all sorts of things because of past disappointments and failures. Because of my husbands unconditional love he was patient and prayerful and God saw us through a difficult time in our relationship. I had never dealt with past hurts, just carried them from one relationship to another.

Unconditional love can make a world of difference. My husband invested a lot of time and exercised a great deal of patience with me and I know it is because he loves me unconditionally.

If you think back on past experiences that caused you hurt or anguish I am sure you will agree that you may have failed to deal with the hurt properly.

When we are hurt we will usually do one of two things, or maybe both. One reaction is to lash out against the pain and the other is to internalize it.

Lashing out may intensify the problem and internalizing it leaves it no where to go. It is difficult for anyone to reason with you as your bitterness is directed towards others. Here we go with that "get even spirit" again. Kept internally, the pain and the hurt just festers and grows like an infectious disease. Not handled properly it can and will destroy you.

My baggage did not only cause me emotional problems but I had physical problems as well. The excess baggage coupled with working almost 30 years for the same employer was a great stress in my life. There were compounded problems as I developed stress related symptoms such as insomnia, weight gain, hypertension, asthma symptoms, acne, bouts of depression and reoccurring illnesses because my resistance was always low. The numerous attacks brought about doctors and more doctors. There was one prescription after another and I was a mess! I was so emotionally challenged there were times I did not know whether I was going or coming. But I thank God for my healing and deliverance! There have been many other painful experiences but it was not until God gave me "Excess Baggage" as a part of my ministry that I have learned how to be free and know it.

Earlier in this chapter there was a brief mention about pain being like a destructive disease. If these experiences are not properly channeled the pain becomes great stresses in your life which will lead to other physical symptoms and illnesses including bitterness and the inflicting of your pain and hurt towards others.

As your faith decreases the pain causes you to lose focus and the enemy sits patiently waiting to devour. He has a lot of time and one of his stronger characteristics is patience. With no focus we have no vision and we cannot serve God effectively. If our vision is vague and not based on the things of God…guess what? It will be on the things of Satan. *Baggage check!*

...Only God can remove this pain.

Dealing with it does not mean that it will not hurt but you can learn how to get total deliverance from it and do it in a way that is spiritually and physically healthy. That is why we have God as our protector and provider. He sent us a Comforter, His Holy Spirit to teach us. Look at John 14:25-27:

"All this I have spoken while still with you. But the Counselor, the Holy Spirit, whom the Father will send in my name, will teach you all things and will remind you of everything I have said to you. Peace I leave with you; my peace I give you. I do not give to you as the world gives. Do not let your hearts be troubled and do not be afraid."(NIV)

Peace...in the midst of turmoil. No one can give the peace we need but the Holy Spirit, the comfort and peace of God that surpasses all our understanding. The world cannot give this peace and neither can the world take it away. Peace is the absence of mental conflict, even in the midst of conflict. That's just like God!

How To Be Free From Excess Baggage

During these painful and challenging times we are never alone. We have comfort in knowing that God's precious Holy Spirit is always with us. Remember we have the peace that Jesus gives, we have the Holy Spirit as Comforter, we have wisdom from the Spirit and we walk not after the flesh but after the Spirit. My God what a blessing!

KNOW *WHO* YOU ARE IN CHRIST

Chapter 7

Know *Who* You Are in Christ

"So God created man in his own image, in the image of God he created him; male and female he created them." Genesis 1:27 (NIV)

Sometimes baggage can result from a very traumatic experience resulting in the control and shaping of ones character which hinders their walk with Christ and disrupts their destiny. In fact, they are so far off course their character will reflect everything but Christ. The impact can be so great that you forget *who* you are in Christ.

A low self-image usually does not evolve over night. It develops during ones childhood, during the formative years. During this period of development the mores of our society as well as the environment affect how we view ourselves. To give an example: If you were called out of your name, talked down to, told you were stupid you grow up believing these things. In which case you will grow up with this negative image of yourself.

How To Be Free From Excess Baggage

No matter what preconceptions you have of yourself because of past experiences, you must remember that we are all created in the image of God. Contrary to how others would have you believe you are not worthless junk. Just because bad things happen to us does not constitute us to be bad people. Bad things do happen to good people.

What is meant by created "in His image?" Until we fell from Grace through the sin of Adam and Eve we had the character of God. It was not until Christ died and rose that we were reconciled to Him. This is why the Bible says if any man be in Christ He is a new creature and all the old things are gone and we are brand spanking new in him. My God! What a savior!

When we accept Christ as our Lord and Savior we become heirs and joint heirs with Him and the greatest of all gifts is eternal life with Him. Our inheritance includes his promises, which are all declared in his Word. So no matter your present situation or condition you are yet victorious because of *who* you are in Christ.

Christ loves us in spite of. He protects us even when we are disobedient. God cares about us and wants us to succeed. In 3 John 2 we find:

Dear friend, I pray that you may enjoy good health and that all may go well with you, even as your soul is getting along well. (NIV)

If your baggage has affected you in such a way that it caused you to be insecure, to make bad decisions or poor choices or, caused you to live a life of sin, it is not too late for Christ to make the difference. Remember in an earlier chapter you said a prayer of repentance and if you meant it God has certainly forgiven you. Do not look back on your failures but instead begin now learning to do the things of Christ, living in holiness.

The Bible provides us with guidelines for Holy living, Colossians 3:1-2 references this.

Since, then, you have been raised with Christ, set your hearts on things above, where Christ is seated at the right hand of God. Set your minds on things above, not on earthly things. For you died, and your life is now hidden with Christ in God. When Christ who is also your life, appears, then you also will appear with him in glory. (NIV)

We must put to death our old fleshly ways, our old earthly nature and put on the "new" which is in Christ Jesus. Our ultimate goal should be to live this life so that we can live again eternally with Christ Jesus. We should strive to walk in his will and in our destiny. The way we can be certain as to what God's will is for our lives is to read and study His Word. The Psalmist David said:

"I have hidden your Word in my heart that I might not sin against you." Psalms 119:11 (NIV)

Because man's innermost nature and deepest feelings lie within his heart, when God's word is imbedded there we can draw from it what we need. It is important for our devotion to be to God. Through the Holy Spirit the word of God teaches, consoles convicts, encourages, leads and guides us.

Personally, I am encouraged and uplifted through the scriptures. All that I need for any situation is in the Word. There is a sense of security when we trust in God. If we dwell in God and He in us we have an inner peace that only God can give.

How To Be Free From Excess Baggage

WHAT IS YOUR EXCESS BAGGAGE?

Chapter 8
What Is Your Excess Baggage?

Now that we have defined excess baggage, discussed the processes of elimination, explained the importance of identifying your baggage and releasing the guilt, traveled the road of denial and realized how to release the hurt and pain, we are ready for the last step. This step leads us to complete freedom and deliverance. *Baggage check!*

This step is very, very important to your complete deliverance. You are going to identify your excess baggage. Here it is essential that you be honest and to do this you must release the pride. If you have not successfully tested the other processes you are not yet ready for your deliverance. We are almost there. Don't you want to be free and know it? Are you tired of your baggage? Don't get this close and let your ego or pride get in the way of your deliverance. If the ego or pride is out of control at this point, you are probably fooled into thinking that you have no baggage and therefore there is not a need for deliverance. You may be more concerned with who you are rather than who you are in Christ. Pride must go!

There was an earlier mention of status being a hindrance. We also discussed how baggage has no respect of persons. Let me share a situation of excess baggage that involved my husband who is an Elder and currently serves as Executive pastor. Ted began preaching at the age of 13 and was licensed in the Church of God in Christ. He is an awesome preacher and teacher and is very astute when it comes to Biblical studies. He never thought one way or the other about excess baggage but he discovered he indeed had baggage.

His biological father walked out of his life when he was about eight years old. The short time he was in his life does not leave him with any fond memories. In fact, whenever he referred to his father it was always "my mother's husband." It was usually in a joking manner but there were some underlying problems, because with the humor there was usually some bitterness expressed. As we talked about it in depth one day, God impressed upon my heart to suggest he make an effort to locate his father and offer forgiveness for his abandoning him as well as bring some closure and reconciliation after years of resentment. His mother was the best resource for getting information and we found in our search that his father was deceased. There were mixed emotions but my husband, after over 40 years released his father, released the pain and was freed from years of bondage caused by excess baggage. It was such an emotional moment. I had never seen my husband cry in such a grieving manner but his tears brought about release from years of unreleased pain and baggage.

I used this example to help those of you who may be hung up behind pride, position or status. If you are desirous of complete deliverance, position and status have to go. Do not allow these things to be an issue because they will just be a hindrance.

Let me remind you that this last step involves total-recall, which may mean reliving the pain as my husband did but this is all right. Your emotions may even rise up to the point of crying but be assured that this is the last time you will ever have to feel this way again. Your deliverance is imminent! You are about to be freed from the negative effects of your baggage forever.

How To Be Free From Excess Baggage

As you recall your baggage, the source of your baggage may be easily and readily identifiable or you may have to think back on things that occurred very early in your life. You may have even suppressed or totally wiped these memories from your conscious mind but subconsciously it is there. It is very important that you take the time now to remember.

At the end of this chapter there is a list for your review that will help you recall your baggage source. You may have more than one source of baggage and this is all right. You are not alone. This list serves as a baggage claim check. But we are not going to hold on to this receipt, we are going to destroy it and it will be gone out of your life forever. As you review the list and find that remembering makes you cry, go ahead and cry. If you find that remembering opens up the pain this is alright too. Remember that this is the last time you will feel this way about this experience. Even during the Excess Baggage seminars I teach this becomes an emotional moment for most of those in attendance. Some have cried, wailed and grieved in pain as they remember how their baggage was destroying them, interfering with their walk with Christ. But one thing is certain and that is their tears unlock the door to their deliverance and they leave delivered and free.

You may have even tried releasing this baggage before and it seems to always find its way back. Confused feelings may be trying to overwhelm you but remember, *"baggage check:"*

"Satan, I am serving notice on you, so get your baggage packed because in the name of Jesus you MUST go!"

This is your time and these moments are very vital to you and your deliverance. This is the exercise I mentioned earlier where folk try to get real sanctified and deep. Remember that position, status and titles will keep you from admitting that you have baggage and you will not be able to see the need for deliverance. If this is you let the pride, status and position go and see what God is going to do in your life. Satan you have to go!

This list is personal and it is not to be reviewed or shared with others. It is your baggage we are dealing with and no one can release it for you but you. No one can deliver you from it but God.

Remember that lying just hinders your complete deliverance and defeats the purpose of the exercise.

Use a separate sheet of paper and make your list using the information from following source list. List the sources that are relevant to you. You can add to your list anything that is not listed. Try doing this exercise during your quiet time when there is most likely not to be any interruptions. Again, remember this is your baggage, only you can honestly identify it and only you can be delivered from it.

SOURCE LIST

[ ] MOLESTATION
[ ] VIOLENT RELATIONSHIP
[ ] CHILD ABUSE

DEATH OF A RELATIVE

[ ] MOTHER
[ ] FATHER
[ ] SISTER
[ ] BROTHER
[ ] AUNT
[ ] UNCLE
[ ] GRANDFATHER
[ ] GRANDMOTHER
[ ] COUSIN
[ ] NEICE
[ ] NEPHEW
[ ] SON
[ ] DAUGHTER

SOURCE LIST CONTINUED

TRAUMA

- [ ] RAPE (KNOWN ATTACKER)
- [ ] RAPE (UNKNOWN ATTACKER)
- [ ] MURDER (YOU WITNESSED)
- [ ] MURDER (YOU CAUSED)
- [ ] VIOLENT ACCIDENT

FEAR OF:

- [ ] DYING
- [ ] WOMEN
- [ ] MEN
- [ ] BEING LOVED
- [ ] GIVING LOVE
- [ ] BEING REJECTED
- [ ] NON-SPECIFIC

PEOPLE BAGGAGE

- [ ] LIED
- [ ] CHEATED

SOURCE LIST CONTINUED

- [ ] MISUSED
- [ ] JEALOUSY
- [ ] SPITEFUL
- [ ] TAKEN ADVANTAGE OF
- [ ] HATEFUL
- [ ] BULLIED
- [ ] DECEIVED
- [ ] VICTIM OF GOSSIP

THINGS YOU DID

- [ ] LIED
- [ ] CHEATED
- [ ] MISUSED
- [ ] JEALOUS
- [ ] SPITEFUL
- [ ] TOOK ADVANTAGE
- [ ] HATED
- [ ] BULLIED
- [ ] DECEITFUL
- [ ] GOSSIPPED
- [ ] ADULTERY

SOURCE LIST CONTINUED

- [ ] IDOLATRY
- [ ] FORNICATION
- [ ] LUST
- [ ] COVETED
- [ ] DISHONEST
- [ ] PAST LIFE

HABITS / ADDICITONS:

- [ ] SMOKING
- [ ] DRINKING
- [ ] PROFANITY / CURSING
- [ ] SUBSTANCE ABUSE / DRUGS
- [ ] PRESCRIPTION ADDICTION

LIST OTHERS:

- [ ] RELIGIOUS TRADITIONS

BE FREE AND KNOW IT!

CHAPTER 9

BE FREE AND KNOW IT!

If you have completed your list you are now ready to leap out of bondage forever. Take a few moments and review your list. Today is your day! If you have honestly listed and come face to face with all of the weights, all of the sources that have held you in bondage, it is time for you to begin walking in your divine destiny. In Acts 14: 8 –10 we find:

In Lystra there sat a man who had been crippled in his feet and was lame from birth. As he listened to Paul speaking Paul looked directly at him and saw that he had faith to be healed and called out, "Stand up on your feet." At that, the man jumped up and began to walk. (NIV)

This is the kind of faith you need as you complete the exercise. Just as the man in the scripture jumped up and began to walk, the evidence of your deliverance will jump up in your spirit because of your faith and belief in God's ability to immediately deliver you even through the power and anointing he has placed on this book.

Review your list for one last time. Now, destroy your list! Shred it, crinkle it, and tear it in tiny pieces. Destroy it! This is your final baggage check. You are back in control with God as your Captain. Now you must believe in your heart and with the information I have given you that you are free from the things you listed. The proof is in God's Word, which has been deposited in your Spirit. Now pray this prayer of confirmation:

"Satan, I am serving you notice because you have complicated my life long enough. I rebuke all confusion, pain and all of the negative feelings and thoughts my baggage has caused me. I release the sources that have tormented me and hindered my walk with Christ. You no longer have control over my life and in the name of Jesus, I rebuke you and the controls you have had over me. In Jesus' name I command you to take your baggage and flee! I am FREE and I KNOW it!"

Look out now! Began to praise and thank God now for your complete deliverance! Hallelujah! If you can believe in your heart that you are free from the bondage of excess baggage, you are free! It will no longer control your emotions, your thought processes nor hinder your walk with Christ. Satan is angry now. He no longer has control over your life nor can he bring these things back to your remembrance causing you pain, anguish, distress, hurt, guilt or insecurity. Now to continue walking in your deliverance you must get on what is called a maintenance program and continually saturate yourself with the Word of God as well as spend quality time in prayer. The closer you walk with God the closer He will walk with you. The following are some scriptural passages from the Bible that serve as conformation and assurance. Read these scriptures daily as you walk in your deliverance.

How To Be Free From Excess Baggage

Words of Comfort & Conformation

Who the Son sets free is free indeed.
(John 8:36) NIV

You have the peace that Jesus gives.
(John 14:25-27) NIV

You have the Holy Spirit as Comforter.
(John 14:15-21) NIV

You have wisdom from the Spirit.
(1 Corinthians 2:6-16)

You walk not after the flesh but after the Spirit.
(Romans 8:1) NIV

Beloved, I wish above all things that you prosper and be in health, even as thy soul prospereth.
(3 John 2) KJV

There hath no temptation to you but such as is common to man: but God is faithful; who will not suffer you to be tempted above that ye are able; but will with temptation also make a way to escape, that ye may be able to bear it. (1Corinthians 10:13) KJV

Wherefore seeing we also are compassed about with so great a cloud of witness, let us lay aside every weight, and the sin, which doth so easily beset us, and let us run with patience the race that is set before us. (Hebrew 12:1)

Therefore being justified by faith, we have peace with God through our Lord Jesus Christ.
(Romans 5:1) KJV

For God hath not given us the spirit of fear, but of power and of love, and of a sound mind.
(2 Timothy 1:7) KJV

WHO THE SON SETS FREE IS FREE INDEED

Rescued from my destruction
Freed from all my sin,
Delivered from my habit
Since I gave my life to Him.

The invincible, the immortal,
The invisible the only God
Who the Son sets free is free indeed.

How To Be Free From Excess Baggage

About The Author

Shiela Yolanda Harris is happily married to Elder Ted Harris, and they both are members of Believers' Christian Fellowship in Los Angeles, California. It is in this ministry and under the leadership of her Senior Pastors, Melvin and April Jackson she accepted her call into the ministry and was licensed as a minister.

Shiela received her Associate of Arts degree in General Studies at East Los Angeles College and her Bachelor of Arts degree in Interdisciplinary Studies, Minor in Public Administration at California State University Dominquez Hills, California.

Shiela is a multi-talented, anointed woman of God. She is the founder of The Young People's Music and Instructional Workshop targeted towards youth, which helps to train and enhance the role that our youth play in the music ministries within our churches. Usually there are well over 100 young people in participation. The workshop has been an annual event since June 1988.

Ambitious and exceptional in their work for the Lord she serves as Lay Pastor and Director of Parish Relations along with her husband who serves as Executive Pastor.

Shiela and her husband Ted are an awesome team. They do the work they love and love the work they do. With all of their many responsibilities they are also the organizers and choreographers for the churches' praise dance team, "Expressions of Praise."

After 30 years of employment Shiela recently retired so she can devote her time to ministry, in her local church as well as in the things God is inspiring her to do. She plans to continue her Biblical studies and education in a School of Ministry, as well as work on a host of projects. God has equipped her with some powerful deliverance teaching for the body of Christ. It is through some of her very own experiences and consequent deliverance that much of her material has been developed. "Excess baggage" is her first publication but it definitely will not be her last.

References

Dictionaries

Strong, James. *The New Strong's Complete Dictionary of Bible Words*. Nashville: Thomas Publishers, 1996

Vine, W.E. *Vine's Complete Expository Dictionary of Old and New Testament Words*. Nashville: Thomas Nelson, Inc., 1996

Merriam-Webster's Collegiate ® Dictionary, Tenth Ed. Principal copyright 1993-Springfield, Mass.

ORDER FORM

To order additional copies of **How To Be Free From Excess Baggage,** complete the information below.

Ship to: (Please Print)

    Name_____

    Address_____

    City,State,Zip _____

Day Phone_____

____No of copies@$12.00 $_____

Postage and handling @
$4.00 per book $_____

Total amount enclosed $_____

Make checks payable to Shiela Y. Harris

Send to: Shiela Y. Harris
 Believers' Christian Ministries
 925 N. Inglewood Ave., #14
 Inglewood, CA 90302